Skateboarding

Skateboarding by **David Hunn**

Contents

© Duckworth 1977

An Alphabook
First published in 1977
by Duckworth, The Old Piano Factory,
43 Gloucester Crescent, London NW1.

ISBN: 0 7156 1248 4 (cloth) 0 7156 1247 6 (paper)

Designed and produced by Alphabet and Image, Sherborne, Dorset,
and printed in England by Chapel River Press, Andover, Hampshire

1 New wheels for old

A skateboard at heart is a short, thin plank with four wheels under it, a kind of elongated roller skate big enough to take both feet. It is a water ski for dry land, a snow ski for asphalt. Ideally, skateboarding is a downhill job, getting its impetus from gravity rather than sweat, but if you want to 'scoot' a board, you can. John Hutson, 21, skateboarded non-stop the 84 miles from San Francisco to Santa Cruz, and that's not all downhill. It took him nearly ten hours.

It provides the latest in downhill thrills, a wild and blissful sensation of free-flowing speed. But it is in the accurate control of such speed that the greatest rewards of the sport lie. Any fool — well, most fools — can stand on a skateboard, or a ski, and be carried away with ever-increasing abandon, culminating in a broken limb for the fool or for the hapless victim he is not smart enough to avoid. The admiration of the bystander is reserved not for that hair-raising hurtler, but for the rider whose sense of direction and balance are so finely tuned that he can slalom his way in and out of obstacles; for the kick turns that are clean, the Christies that are clear, the handstands that are steady.

For those who are mastering the art ahead of the rush, skateboarding now provides an unparalleled opportunity for exhibitionism of the best kind, for self-fulfilment equalled only by the golfer who at last cures himself of the hook, or the swimmer who learns how to breathe without disturbing a front crawl. If you can ride a skateboard, and ride it so it looks as if God shod your feet with ballbearings, then you are in. You are hot. You are very pleased with yourself, are you not?

How did it all begin? Even from such short range, it is hard to be absolutely sure. Almost certainly it was in California, among the young surf riders who somehow manage to spend their years on the Pacific coast without actually doing much about earning a living. Though it is an extension of roller skating, that sport does not seem to have been involved in its growth; and indeed when you ride a board, you realise it has little to do with that humdrum activity. In its art and its craft, skateboarding has much more in common with surfing and with snow skiing, with the advantage that all you need as a playground is a hard, fairly smooth surface with a slope.

Its birth in California was the crude wedding of a short surfboard and roller skate wheels. The time at which public consciousness took it in, 1965. It flared, illuminated the neighbourhoods, spluttered and was gone in a year, though in that time they say fifty million boards were sold. Gone, that is, as a rage, a fad. Some never gave it up, but it remained a private pastime, waiting for technology to light the fuse again. That took nearly ten years, but when it happened the explosion was deafening. By the end of 1975 the American magazine *Time*, not one inclined to inflate balloons, reported that southern California was in the grip of a revival as frantic as any ever whipped up by an evangelist. Already, they estimated, there were thirty million skateboarders in the States, and southern California's two million were increasing by 5,000 a day.

What sort of miracle was it that exhumed the corpse of skateboarding? The injection was made, unwittingly at the time, by a freshman engineering student at the Virginia Polytechnic Institute (subsequently, as you might expect, tagged by *Time* as a 'dropout'). Frank Nasworthy was his name, aged 24 then, and what he was working on between lectures was the possibility of putting plastic wheels on roller skates. Up to then, they had been made of metal, hard rubber, clay or a composition mixture, which was just what the skateboard wheels of the first era were made of also. All right for roller skating on wooden rinks, but the much heavier wear caused by skateboarding at high speeds on asphalt or concrete was too much for them. 'I used to wear out four of the old composition wheels a day,' recalled a veteran in *Skateboarder* magazine. 'I used to go down to the roller rink in Santa Barbara, and they'd sell me four used wheels for a buck. I thought that was the greatest deal in the world.'

'The old wheels just weren't making it,' said another, writing on 'Skateboarding in the dark ages'. 'They'd get hot and fall off, or to pieces, or come to any number of other unforeseen ends. The sport was virtually discarded even as it suffered its birthpangs.' Apart from other hazards, the wheel and truck assembly was so rigid and so unstable that it was said the rider was liable to come off if he ran into a cigarette end. Certainly a pebble spelt disaster, much as a stone might have done to a motor car with wooden wheels.

So what about Nasworthy's plastic? With $700 he saved by working in a restaurant, he formed the Cadillac Wheels Company, and with Creative Urethanes Incorporated providing the technical know-how, began producing cast-moulded polyurethane wheels for roller skaters in 1968. In this process, the liquid plastic is poured into the mould cavity and cured in kilns for 20 minutes. It produced a wheel of marvellous durability and great holding power, but as far as expert roller skaters were concerned, it was a washout. The comparatively soft wheels

Tony Alva

were too slow for a sport in which nothing much mattered but getting round the track first.

Because of the dormant state of skateboarding, it was five years before the Cadillac company thought of introducing their new wheels to those old boards. Once they did, it was like the first car with air in its tyres. 'We couldn't believe it,' someone said. 'It was Christmas every day. It was sunrise for ever.' Whatever you did with them, the wheels lasted. However you punished them, they held the track — which is why in California today you can see skateboarders riding round the *walls* of empty swimming pools, right up to the rim. It is why the boldest and the best among them can,

when they get the chance, ride the inside of vast drainage tunnels, and still be on their boards when they are over halfway up.

That is what the urethane wheel did for skateboarding, and the sport responded with an alacrity that was almost overwhelming. At about the same time as Nasworthy's triumph, and quite independently, another wheel of similar construction, the Metaflex, matured through injection moulding. Here the urethane is injected into the mould under high pressure and intense heat, producing a harder wheel of more perfect shape, but a slightly lower quality of traction. Between them, Cadillac and

Metaflex rocked the industry. Even the defunct *Skateboarder* magazine took a couple of excited breaths and leaped from the grave, selling (at a dollar a time) 75,000 copies of the first new issue and 100,000 of the second. Now it is a must for skateboarders, six times a year.

'Two hundred years of American technology has unwittingly created a massive cement playground of unlimited potential. But it was the minds of 11 year olds that could see that potential.' Another piece of accurate skateboarding philosophy from the States. The truth of it you can see for yourself if you are within reach of any one of the

pockets of the sport today. Down the mighty Broad Walk of Kensington Gardens in London, almost within sight of the statue of Peter Pan, there sweeps (when the custodians are busy elsewhere) an irregular echelon of kids, some looking hardly old enough to be out on their own. The thin, swift rumble of urethane on asphalt bounces between ground and board and rushes joyously out from a dozen youngsters. This is kids' stuff, and there are a few about who would like it kept to their back gardens. Perambulating nannies who fear for the safety of their straying toddlers; pensive parents who cannot believe these juvenile exhibitionists can possibly reach the gate without injury.

Watch them and you soon appreciate that the natural aptitude of the really young for such delicate activity is as great as it is for skiing. The lack of fear which is their gift takes them halfway to success before they begin. Their agility, flexibility, instinct and grace complete the job. It was little seedlings like these who took the sport up in the first Californian boom of the mid-1960s, and who were still young enough to pick it up again in the rebirth of 1975. It is these dazzling young exponents, in London or Brighton or Newquay or Glasgow or wherever else boards roll, who will take skateboarding on to elder brothers and sisters, to an age group better suited to exploit its intricacies.

feel yourself rocking from side to side. The most stable and safe way, and the one that gives you best control, is to ride with your feet across the board, one over each axle. The line of your shoulders will not be exactly that of the direction of travel, but slightly inclined one way or the other, depending which side you find it natural to lead with. Like boxers, most lead with the left. If you do, you and the board will be pointing straight ahead, to 12 on the clock, and your left shoulder will be pointing to 11.

A word about shoes: wear them. Bare-footed board riders do exist — they say it gives them more sensitive control — but they tend to be scar-footed

2 Now push off

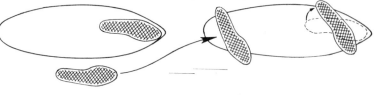

Have you ever tried to teach anybody to ride a bicycle? There is not much you can tell them, is there, except that pretty soon they will stop falling off and wonder what they were ever making such a fuss about? Skateboarding is much the same. If it looks easy to you when you watch it, you will have no problem at all. If you are nervous about setting off down your first little slope, you will soon lose your balance — but you will soon get over that. The problems do not begin until you come off at speed, but no beginner should be so foolish as to plunge down the sort of slope that blurs the edges of the scenery.

Do not make the common mistake of supposing that the safest way of starting is with your feet pointing down the board, one behind the other, like a water skier. It seems to be a natural inclination, but resist it. As soon as you are on, you will

riders. Dedicated skateboarders in the States say they get through a pair of shoes a week, but better that than a pair of feet. It is not only the soles from which you are likely to lose skin, however tough they are, but the toes and upper surfaces too, when your own board runs over you. So some tough, lightweight shoes are essential, flat-soled, to enable you to change position on the board with the minimum disturbance. Go for crepe, rubber, or a composition sole with a good grip, and if you can find something with a reinforced toe, so much the better. Many riders like as little over the foot as possible, but experts recommend a canvas boot, or at least a shoe with ankle support.

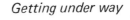

Getting under way

While we are on the subject, and before you push off on your first trip, what about gloves? You will not see many British youngsters wearing them, but in California you will, and special gloves for the sport are on the market there. As you get more experienced, you will find there are a lot of tricks that bring your hands very close to the ground, and even before that, admit it, you are going to fall off now and then. When you do, you are usually going to put out your hands to save yourself. Asphalt burn can be very painful. Why not wear an old pair of leather gloves that are not much good for anything else, or better still, one of those pairs of cheap industrial gloves you can buy from an iron-monger or hardwear store? Later, we shall be considering the more thorough forms of protection you will need if you move on to big-time skateboarding.

Now you are set to go, poised on the brink of a gentle asphalt slope. Please do not underestimate the force of gravity and the momentum you will shortly gather. Try to find a slope that is short as well as not too steep — it will be less far to walk back, anyway. Push off with what is going to be your rear foot. Your front foot will be in position over the front axle, though during this preliminary movement it will need, as you will immediately discover, to be pointing not straight across the board, but on the diagonal. When you are under way, swing the rear foot into its position over the rear axle; and having got there, you may want to adjust the front foot into a position parallel with the rear foot — whatever position gives you the most control.

9

Settle yourself comfortably as you move, your weight evenly distributed. Knees gently bent, body relaxed and inclined forward, arms slightly in front of you. Let it take you. (There is nobody about, is there? You are not doing this on a road used by cars, are you?) It depends how happy and confident you feel on the board how soon you begin to experiment with steering. When you do, let it be at the bottom, when the slope has levelled out. You will soon find that changing direction on a skateboard is no harder than it is on a bicycle. It is a matter of leaning, of gently changing the distribution of weight from dead centre, to one side or the

other. If you are riding with your left side forward, a slight sway out with your backside will put the pressure on the left side of the board and take it off the right, and the board will veer to the left as those wheels bite harder into the surface. Lean the other way, and you will go right. The amount by which you transfer your weight to one side of the board or the other controls the degree of veer you can expect, but don't think you can make a sharp turn like this, any more than you could on skis or a bicycle. There comes a time when you have to use the handlebars, and when you have to execute a kick turn.

Before you do, you might consider stopping, or at least getting off in a hurry, which no doubt you will soon need to do. The basic rule is almost too obvious to state: if you have to step off at speed, you must step in the direction of travel, just as you would if you had to jump off a bus before it had stopped. Otherwise, there is going to be a sharp argument between your legs and the ground on the subject of where you were going before you hopped off, and your legs are going to lose. So you step off parallel to the board and run with it as long as necessary to bring yourself to a halt and to stop the board.

This is important, and it is not just a matter of having to go to the bottom of the hill to get the board back. Though you may have found a secluded spot today, there will later be times when pedestrians are about. They will not relish an unattended skateboard cracking them in the ankle. Remember, these are dangerous instruments when they are out of control, with you on the board or without you. It is up to you to control them at all times, and to see that you are not a menace, or even a nuisance, to the public. The sport has enough problem finding suitable tracks already, and it cannot afford to antagonize the ratepayers.

Okay, you have had a few sessions on your nursery slope, got the hang of steering, nipped off at speed a few times. You have fallen over once or twice, taken the skin off the ball of your thumb because you thought it was cissy to wear gloves, and got a nasty graze down your left forearm (see Chapter 6 on first aid hints). Now you are interested in kick turns, so go down to the bottom where it is flat. While you are there, practise a bit of shunting first. That is the skateboarding name for what we referred to earlier as scooting — one foot on the board, the other pushing, a manoeuvre that guy must have used a lot during his 84 mile trip in California.

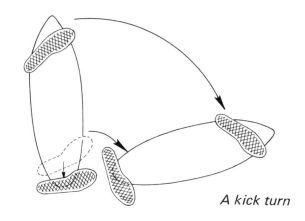

A kick turn

You will discover for yourself what seems to be the most comfortable way of doing this, but what you must aim at is to keep your weight over the board, whichever foot you use; otherwise you will not be able to keep a straight path. The foot needs to be straight down the board, the heel over the rear axle, and obviously, as you shove with your leg, your onboard one must give a little at the knee to enable you to reach the ground comfortably. Try to achieve a steady rhythm, and practise using either foot. After a while you will sort out how to change feet without stopping the board, just by bringing the pushing foot on to the board over the front axle and removing the rear one. Once you have done that, shunting becomes a pleasant, useful and relaxing exercise. In the skateboarding States, lots of older people are doing it instead of jogging — that ambling run that is supposed to keep the signs of middle-age at bay. To quote one of the intense experts of *Skateboarder* magazine, 'To experience the jog is to experience a fluid discovering of propelling motion generated from small amounts of exerted energy.' No doubt he is right.

Kick turning Try it first on a static board, until you get the measure of the movement. Your rear foot must move back, to the tail of the board. Shift almost all your weight to that foot, and let the front wheels rise off the ground. As they do, turn the nose of the board quite sharply through 90 degrees. The easier turn to master is the one in which the board moves in the direction your front foot is pointing, but remember this is a movement that is guided, not inspired, by the front foot: the turn comes from the hips. You will need some practice to do this properly, both the 'push' and the 'pull' kick turns, and when you think you have them slick, get under way with shunting and try them again before you go up the slope at all. Do not attempt a kick turn at speed until you are more experienced — you will find the board will turn, but you will go straight on.

How long it takes you to master the basic manoeuvres depends on your natural ability and on how much time you spend practising. When you are really familiar with kick turns, you will not find **tic-tac** too difficult. This is a means of propulsion on the flat by incessant half-turns in either direction alternately, rather in the way that boatmen can propel a skiff by waggling one oar over the stern from side to side. Keep your rear foot well back, as for a kick turn, and move the nose of the board

about 30 degrees to one side and 30 degrees to the other, to and fro. You do not need to lift the nose as high as you do for a full kick turn, and you will find, abracadabra, that the board edges forward quite well, even up a slight slope if you work at it. It will take you a week or two to perform all those functional manoeuvres satisfactorily. After that, you come to the part of skateboarding that makes it so exciting: the totally unnecessary, entirely captivating, area of tricks, of showmanship. Before we plunge too deeply into that classy side of the business, try a little exercise that gives you a big kick: **crouching.** Asked why he did it, one lad replied: 'It feels better.' You will know what he

meant when you try it. As you go down into the crouch, you will need to adjust your basic foot position so both feet are pointing at least half forward. You are facing forward, your arms held in front of you, both to help keep your balance and to reduce wind resistance.

By crouching, you are presenting a much smaller surface to the wall of air ahead of you, and you will find your speed increases appreciably. It is important to ensure you are perfectly balanced: you have now brought yourself down very close to that hard road that is flashing by under your nose, and if you topple over, you have little chance of avoiding it. But don't worry, you have lowered your centre of gravity, which is in itself a secure and useful thing to do.

3 Nuts and bolts

A skateboard consists of three distinct components: chassis, trucks and wheels. Though it is sensible to buy a complete assembly in the first place, the wide range of accessories now available enables the skateboarder to switch later to something that may better suit his style or his intentions — wheels that are softer, for better traction, or wider, for greater stability, or bigger in circumference, for speed; trucks that are higher, or more manoeuvrable, or with longer axles; a chassis (which in most cases is no more than the board itself) that may have some of a dozen different characteristics. The subtleties of these are not of great importance in the early stages, when you should be looking for a board that is not too long, not too narrow, not too flexible, but just right.

The experts may have five or ten different skateboards, according to what they are aiming to do at the time. But in the same way that most of us get by with just one tennis racquet and not the armful you see being carried on at Wimbledon, so one skateboard will be enough for quite a while. It is also likely to be as much as you can afford: at the time of writing, the boards made by just one of the most reputable firms in the United States range in price from $30 to $60 complete. American boards are selling in Britain from £12–£60, and the much less efficient British product at £15.

The basic division of boards is between stiff and flexible, with every intermediate degree catered for. The truly rigid board is all-wood, made probably of oak, birch, ash or mahogany. It absorbs vibration more efficiently than a fibreglass board, and so is in demand by the speed skater. It is also heavier, and offers a more stable platform for advanced tricks such as handstands, headstands and high jumps, and has the advantage of being a much easier chassis on which to change trucks. But a wooden board is less workable. It does not respond to what is called 'weighting' and 'unweighting', the pressure and relief of pressure applied by the body at strategic moments to a flexible board in a kind of pumping action. A flexible board, usually made of either solid or laminated fibreglass, replies to weighting with 'punch', a reflex in which the board snaps back to its original shape.

When it does so swiftly from a deep flex, it is said to have a good 'memory'.

By using the correct pumping technique, a flexible skateboard will accelerate through turns, and can also be propelled on the flat. An ideal amount of flex would be up to half an inch when you are standing on the board, and twice as much when you are applying pressure to it. One firm manufactures a board called Powerflex, which they claim can take a weight of two tons without breaking. In the hope of proving it, their advertisements show one bent nearly double under the weight of an elephant's foot.

The length of skateboards varies within the normal limits of 24 to 30 inches, to the unusual ones of 21½ inches and 3, 4 or even 5 feet. Width choice is seldom offered within one manufacturer's range, the standards generally being between 6 and 7½ inches. Kick-tails have become popular, a turn-up at the rear of the board that makes most manoeuvres

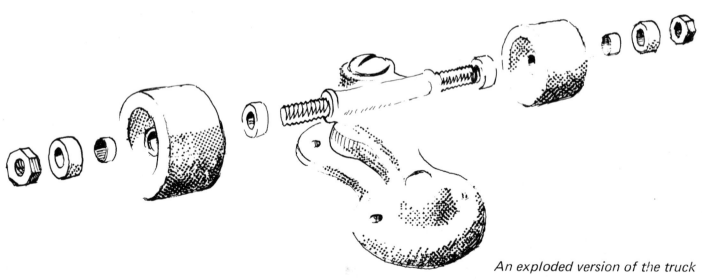

An exploded version of the truck

easier but some more difficult, and in their search for variety the makers are now producing noses that turn up as well (double kick), and even some that turn down. Some decks are psychedelically coloured, for which you pay, some are textured to give a better grip, some have textured tape stuck on them. With such a choice, and with the style of board being as individual a matter as the style of bicycle, it is hard to give dogmatic advice to a beginner. Most go for a moderately flexible fibreglass board, 26 or 27 inches long.

When you come to wheels, the choice is legion. Urethane is a must, but they vary in circumference from 1½ to 2¾ inches, and in width from 1½ to 3 inches, or even to a roller the full width of the board. The wheel bearings are of vital importance to the highly-developed rider, and they come in three basic grades: open, sealed, and precision. In the last the bearings do not touch each other and the wheels move almost silently, with less than usual vibration. Wheels, known as slicks in racing circles, are easily removable from the axles round which they revolve. The axle, usually made of hardened steel, is part of the other vital ingredient of a skateboard, the truck.

This steel or aluminium alloy mechanism weds each pair of wheels to the board, holding the middle of the axle in a way that permits a degree of turn and rock. The amount of movement varies with the type of truck, and the expert skateboarder balances very carefully the precise qualities of the speed and traction of his wheels, the manoeuvrability of his trucks and the flexibility of his board. Fibreglass boards, which tend to pass on rather than absorb vibration, are often fitted with quarter-inch or half-inch rubber shock-absorber pads between the truck and the board. On a wooden board, the position of the trucks is capable of adjustment.

In your early stages you are not going to be too

concerned with such niceties. What you want is a strong, comfortable and efficient board. Read on and you will understand why the hot riders of southern California need precise perfection from their boards, and why many of them list in their wardrobe reinforced gloves, a heavily-padded impact jacket and a crash helmet.

4 Seeking the high spots

The world skateboarding speed record is rather more than 60 miles an hour. The high jump record is 4 feet 8 inches, but we will come to that later. The Pacific coast is packed with people who can skateboard off pavements on their hands and off tables on their feet, and there are one or two who, given a chance, will jump over a car. Riding up the walls of tunnels and swimming pools, as we saw earlier, is common practice among high-grade boarders, and so is negotiating a downhill slalom course with incredible accuracy and frightening speed.

Guy Grundy

The inevitable but unforseen development of such expertise and ambition in the States has brought problems, and the same ones have already been tasted in Britain. Nobody may object to a young skateboarder rolling gently down an incline on a deserted no-thoroughfare, but they will care if he roars down the pavement on which they are walking, or the park path where they were enjoying the peace. Where to take your boards has become a major problem in many areas, particularly for those who need more than the average amount of space to exercise their talents. When new 'hot spots' have been discovered in America, the word has carefully been passed round only to the local hot set, and some surprising venues are among them. One young group visits a multi-storey car park in Washington early every Sunday morning, steaming from floor to floor and slaloming round the pillars. In New York City, where the sale of skateboards has been illegal since the summer of 1975, some young boarders responded by making some unheralded bursts across the concourse of Grand Central Station.

It is in California that the sheer mass of skateboarders makes it difficult to find good spots, despite the vast space in that state. The numbers of riders have persuaded some city councils to get really tough with the sport. San Diego, for instance, started by imposing a $55 fine for skateboarding on public roads, and has now made it illegal on all streets and pavements and parks, and it is the same in Long Beach. Some schools have made special provision to accommodate what is probably the most popular sport among their pupils, but some have gone the other way and banned it entirely (you can hardly blame some of them, who found themselves sued by parents for negligence when their kids hurt themselves).

Out in the no man's land between the hills and

19

the sea, skateboarding seekers found a great concrete drainage tunnel, 200 yards long, perfectly round, and some 15 feet in diameter. Dodge the guards in the maintenance yards, duck the barbed wire, turn your head when you pass the notice 'No Skateboarding, Subject to fine — US Code 641' and you are on to a great time. Or you were, until the police moved in. They built up to a peak of twenty arrests a night and then used a helicopter to help them close the place down.

Then there was that unbelievable trip crudely known to skateboarders as 'The Toilet Bowl'. This is drainage too, as you might expect, in a canyon out in the hills behind Hollywood. Not the place to visit in the rainy season, but in the long dry summer there was probably no more famous skateboarding hot spot in the whole of the United States. From the top it is rather like looking down a shallow loo, with at the bottom a huge vertical pipe and the end of a three-foot tunnel. The whole thing is shaped just like a lavatory bowl, about 75 feet across the top and 35 feet deep in the centre. Not a regular funnel shape, because the middle bit is hellishly steep and at the top it is a bit more tolerable. It was the scene of the world's wildest board riding, until the Los Angeles city council took a look. Then the council spent $12,000 of the residents' money in lacing the entire surface with speed bumps, so you could not even ride it on a bicycle.

Skateboarding has, to a small degree, reached South Africa and some countries of Western Europe, but in Australia it is big business. There was once some pressure on the government to ban it. The prime minister of the time said, in effect: 'Not on your nellie! If I were a kid, I'd want to ride one.' So the big cities are building special sites for skateboarders, which is just what the sport needs and deserves. They are coming in California

too, with skateparks either open or on the way in Los Angeles, Ventura, Carlsbad, San Gabriel and San Fernando. These are totally and scientifically man-made efforts, varying in size between half an acre and two acres and containing just about every sort of terrain a good rider wants, as well as nursery areas for beginners.

It is too much to hope that anything as elaborate as that will appear in Britain for a few years. Until they do — and for sure they would be commercial propositions — the ever-increasing horde of young participants will be forced to take their boards just where they should not, to the streets and public paths. Skateboarding cannot be suppressed by legislation, any more than soccer was squashed by Henry VIII. It is too buoyant. It will burst out all over.

Frank Nasworthy, by the way, the guy who first introduced the polyurethane wheel to skateboarders, has his own skateboarding ramp that he takes round for exhibitions by the Bahne/Cadillac team. It rises to 12 feet, is 24 feet wide and 150 feet long, weighs 10 tons and includes slalom courses with electric starting gates. Competition is as earnest in skateboarding as it is in skiing, with championships in freestyle (tricks), slalom and speed boarding sponsored by many of the leading manufacturers. They all enter teams of riders who are contracted to them, for which the skaters (of both sexes) often get not only free equipment but an attractive financial inducement. Some are full-time professionals, living from exhibitions and instruction. Many of the most successful part-timers have become heroes through the publicity given to their achievements by Press coverage and, particularly, by advertising, which is enormous and highly competitive. What is it that they can do that makes them so special? It is time for a look at the way the other half skates.

Power-assisted catamaran

Slalom

24

5 Riding high

SLALOM This is the steering of a course, usually downhill, between 'gates' or in and out of markers, so plotted that the skateboarder must ride a tight zig-zag line from beginning to end. As in skiing, it is ridden against the clock, and the most successful slalom riders are those who can most finely judge the shortest line to take and maintain it without losing speed in the turns. For practice, it is useful to run imaginary slaloms, fixing a line in your mind at the top of the hill and keeping to it in the unbroken rhythm that is essential to high speed.

The technique is based on weighting and unweighting, the pressing down on the board and the relaxing of pressure that is the basis of all steering. The unweighting process is greatly helped by using a flexible board that snaps back into shape when you cease bearing down on it. The purpose of the pressure is to force the wheels, on one side or the other, into closer contact with the ground, thus increasing the friction and slowing the rate at which those wheels revolve. This obviously causes the board to turn towards that side, so as you

Slalom

used), returning upright between markers and swinging the other way almost immediately. Beware, though, of exaggerated body movement: it will quickly lead to loss of control. The position of the feet in slalom is, as usual, a personal matter. Some place one behind the other and some have them almost side by side, but a good suggestion until you find a better one is to place your leading foot straight down the board, toes over the front axle, and keep the rear foot at right angles to it, across the board.

approach each marker, you must weight the side nearer to it. This should be completed by the time you are level with the marker, when unweighting should immediately begin. By then, you will be heading for the far side of the next marker, so unweighting on one side leads directly to weighting on the other, and so on. The rhythm is ceaseless and exciting.

Watching top-rate slalom riders at work, you will see that the upper part of the body is leaning over each marker (ordinary plastic road cones are often

SPEED Never attempt a slope so steep or so long that it is going to take you out of control. Concentrate first on achieving the maximum speed on a slope that you know is comfortably within the limits of your technique and your equipment. Equipment first: make sure your bearings are clean and lubricated, and all the nuts and screws of your truck are really tight. The vibration caused by a loose truck is magnified alarmingly at high speed, and can set up 'high speed wobble', a condition from which it is almost impossible to recover. If you

are using a fibreglass board, fit it with rubber shock-absorbers. Finally, equip yourself properly. Make sure your body is completely covered, and padded at danger points.

Choose an incline with no traffic, few skateboarders and plenty of stopping space at the end of the hill. The cleaner and smoother the surface, the better your control will be. As soon as you push off from the top, begin pumping the board, with rhythmic weighting and unweighting that is this time equally distributed over the board. This will give you early acceleration. Having built up your speed, streamline your body by crouching, extending your arms straight in front of you as if you were diving, and dipping your head between them. Even on your ordinary practice slope, this technique will give you a positively faster run. Near the bottom, stand up to increase your wind resistance and help the braking. These are the points recommended by Denis Shufeldt, a 26 year old yoga instructor from San Diego, who is consistently the fastest skateboarder in the world — though not, at this moment, the world record holder.

First and last, do remember this piece of advice from him, expressed in *Skateboarder* magazine: 'It's clear to me that high speeds should not be attempted by a novice skateboarder. An experienced skater is well aware of the possibilities of broken bones, or being ground into hamburger if a collision with the asphalt occurs.'

27

TRICKS Earlier, we explored the basic manoeuvres of skateboarding. Now we come to those that stop the passer-by in his tracks, the flashy tricks of the game that are as natural a part of your development as a skateboarder as they are in the related sports of water and snow skiing, gymnastics and trampolining. You want to be good at your sport, and once you have mastered the basics, the proper way to extend yourself is to attempt the advanced techniques — but gently and sensibly, in a safe place, and with proper body protection.

Nose to tail 180 Known also as the *ro-lo*, this is an extension of the kick-turn you learned earlier. This time the turn is of 180 degrees, and again and

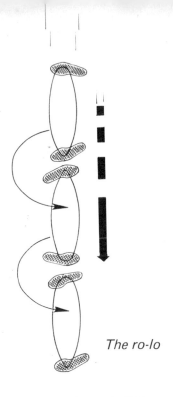

The ro-lo

again: a succession of 180s, nose to tail, tail to nose. If accurately done, you continue to advance in a straight line, but it takes some getting used to, since every time you turn you are facing the other way. You need to concentrate to maintain your balance and your rhythm. Once you have it, you can keep it up as long as your legs can take it.

Christie A spectacular crouching trick requiring a great flair for balance and a determination not to think how close to the ground is your head. If ever you needed a helmet, it is with this one, and even Shufeldt, who has given his name to one of the most difficult Christie variations, wears one when he performs it. Assuming you lead with your left side, place your left foot well down the board and your right hand well along the board. In the full crouch position, straighten your right leg so it

*Rocky Brann executes
a neat Royal Christie*

is coming away from the board at about two o'clock in relation to your direction of travel, and balance it with your left arm held out on the other side. That one is known as the Royal Christie, and like the others, not the least difficult part is getting into and out of the position on the move.

For a full-extension Christie, both hands are off the board, the arms extended at the sides. To see a gang of young Americans demonstrating this one, with the left hand and even the backside barely off the ground, is enough to cause casualty departments to cancel all leave, and to give their mothers heart failure. Shufeldt's particular torture, known as the Shu-fly Christie, requires you to perform the full extension with the wrong leg. That is, your right (rear) foot is on the front of the board and the left (front) foot is extended diagonally across the direction of travel, with the left thigh braced against the right shin. If that does not sound any more difficult than the standard full-extension, wait till you try it.

Wheelies As if it was not enough to remain upright and in control on a four-wheel descent, you are now required to do so on two only, nose or tail. Try tail first, moving back on the board until the front wheels leave the ground. The ideal is to reach a position in which the board is perfectly balanced, the tail just clear of the ground (a kick-tail board is helpful here) and the nose well up. Your feet must be so placed that you can weight on either side for steering as usual.

The same principles apply to the more difficult nose wheelies, with both feet this time on the front of the board. In a tail wheelie, if your board

touches the ground all you will do is to lose some board. On the nose, you will probably lose some toe and maybe some face as well, as the board is liable to tip up as abruptly as a bicycle with a stick in its front spokes. With either of them, once you have found the balance point, turn your attention to style, which is what separates the men from the boys in most tricks. Your knees should be slightly bent, your arms either right up beside your ears or horizontal from the shoulders, your body slightly arched. It is a good feeling when you get it, and there is more to come. You can now move on to experiment with one-footed nose or tail wheelies, and to refine those with what you do with the spare foot.

Moving on to the outrageously exotic, there is the squatting wheelie, in which you slowly crouch all the way to the board while doing a normal wheelie; the nose-to-tail wheelie, in which the front foot is across the nose of the board and the rear foot across the tail, and you delicately rock from one to the other as you go; and the daffy two-board wheelie, that few are confident to attempt: your leading foot performs a tail wheelie on the front board, your trailing foot a nose wheelie on the rear board. Do your best to keep the boards close together, otherwise you split straight up the middle. Finally, something more like a circus act than a skateboarding trick, but it has been done; a one-footed nose wheelie on a board that is itself balanced on another board. Don't try it.

A two-board nose wheelie

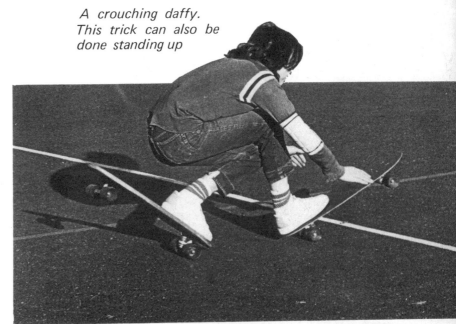

A crouching daffy.
This trick can also be
done standing up

Handstands Once you have seen one, you will not be happy till you are upside down too, though you may care to note that some skateboarders resent the intrusion of a gymnastic exercise into their mobile sport. Ideally, you need a flat, blunt-nosed board and one that is not too long, as the recommended procedure is to grip the ends of the board, your knuckles facing more or less fore and aft. It will immediately occur to you that there is probably no more certain way in the world of tearing chunks out of your fingers other than actually feeding them into a mincing machine, and you are so right. Whatever your friends advise or the pictures show, please do not try handstands without gloves. That said, it is probably easier to do a handstand on a moving, stable board than on the ground, in the same way that it is easier to stay on a bicycle when it is moving than when it is not. Start on a slope, seizing the board and giving yourself two or three crab-like steps for impetus. Then kick up your legs, lock your elbows and look where you are going. It is rated smarter to keep your legs vertical, though most travel with the body arched.

As you belt down, to the admiration and terror of the neighbourhood, it will at some point strike you that an emergency stop will not be the easiest of procedures. True, but it is surprising how easy some make it look. Obviously, you must get your feet back to the ground as soon as possible, and the classy way to do that is in a cartwheel motion, bringing the board with you. If that does not work for you, come back to earth the same way you went up, but you must half turn as you hit the ground in order to run on and lose your momentum. Again, keep hold of the board.

Developing from the handstand are the elbow stand, the headstand and the double-board handstand. For the first, the whole forearm up to the elbow takes the weight, with the hands gripping the sides of the tail of the board and the forearms side by side down the board. The headstand is certainly best performed with a helmet and on a rigid board. The hands grip the sides, the head nestles firmly at the tail end. Remember, for both elbow and head stands, you must be facing backwards when you are on your feet at the start; otherwise when you are on your head you will be looking where you have just been, not where you are going.

If you can do all that and are just plain bored, try the handstand on two boards, one behind the other, a hand flat across the width of each one. Or, on one board, a stand on one hand and one finger. Yes, some do. But then there are some who do

nose or tail wheelies in the handstand position, but others agree you might just as well donate your fingers straightaway to the hamburger shop.

Back-boarding It is not as dangerous as it looks to ride the board on your back. Lie across the board, your bottom just behind the front truck. You use your stomach muscles to keep your head and shoulders up out of harm's way, and to control your weighting of the board — which is not easy. Spread your weight as evenly as possible, and do not try to get up until the run has finished.

Back-boarding

Bench jumps The term covers all drops in flight – off bench, table, pavement, anything like that. Start low, a pavement is plenty. Aim to lift the nose of the board at least a couple of inches as you go, as if you wanted to land on your rear wheels alone. If you let the nose hit the ground first, you will be liable to tip up. Most important of all, keep the board from tipping sideways as you drop. If you land on your outside wheels alone, on either side, you may be heading for a broken ankle. Make sure your trucks are tight, as slack screws will be aggravated by the continual impact. It is no great problem, while you are at it, to learn to mount pavements. Simply weight down on the tail till the nose wheels are clear of the kerb — but watch the timing.

High jumps Very exciting, very difficult. You take off from the board in motion, clear the bar, and land on the board again. Is it possible? So much so that 4 feet 4 inches has been cleared several times. As in a conventional high jump, you need two uprights to support a very light crossbar, so placed that it will come off as soon as you hit it. You must wear shoes, and any other protective clothing that does not hamper you too much; this is a trick in which nobody escapes without a fall now and then. Avoid a very flexible board. Your object is to approach the bar at a steady speed, moderate to slow, take off with a spring light enough not to dis-

Clearing the bar at 4 feet 3 inches

turb the passage of the board, clear the bar and land on the board without upsetting it or yourself.

Think only of jumping for height. The distance you need, in order to pass over the bar, will be achieved automatically, thanks to your momentum at the moment of take-off. The precise moment of the jump is something you can only decide by experience, and varies according to your speed, but remember that most people jump too soon. This forces them to try and make more distance than should be necessary, and the effort of so doing often retards the progress of the board, which will then be not quite where you want it when you return to earth. Only practice will teach you this timing, probably the most difficult art in skateboarding to acquire.

The two most important points to remember: jump only for height, and don't attempt to land on the board if you can see you are not going to land squarely on it. This is even more difficult to accomplish than clearing the bar. The novice will find it useful to start by jumping up and down on a static board, getting the hang of the light-footed take-off, and to follow this by jumping in motion, but without using a bar. A few dummy runs like that will not only help the technique, but give you a fair idea where to put the bar when you do start to use one. Don't advance too fast: wait till you clear one height nine times out of ten before you move on to the next. Even one of the world's experts, who has cleared 4 feet 3 inches several times, is still concentrating on being infallible over 4 feet.

The long jump is a technical variation of the high jump. Carried out at a much greater speed, though not downhill, it requires a similar determination not to think about the length, just the height. The speed at take-off, plus the height, will determine the length of your jump.

jumps

*Bryan Beardsley
over a car*

Torger Johnson rising to the rim

Olly Haycraft bank riding

Bowl riding This is the great kick in California, but you will be hard pressed to find that sort of private swimming pool in Britain — and one that is both empty and deserted. American pools, which are about as common as lawn mowers, tend to be exotically curved, and the floor merges with the walls in another curve. The skateboarder gets up enough speed to run up the wall a bit, increasing speed as he comes down again so that next time he goes higher. The experts raise such a speed that they

can run up to the top of an eight-foot wall, at which point their bodies, briefly, are horizontal. This is something that could never be attempted with the old, hard composition wheels, but has become an incredible reality with polyurethane.

The crucial part of the trick, apart from summoning enough nerve to try it, is to come down the wall in one piece. If you hang up there just half a second too long, the traction of your wheels will fail and you have a considerable problem.

Though skateboarders outside America may never have the chance to use a pool like this, you can sometimes find some concrete banking suitably placed. If the sides and floor do not merge smoothly, it is quite possible, at a fair speed, to mount such a bank, making a turn at the top. Bank riding of this kind is becoming more popular as skateboarders find sloping walls as shown on page 41.

Walking the board Complicated to explain, but not so bad to perform. You are on the board in the normal riding position, feet across the axles, leading with the left side. Try this one on a gentle slope at first, and one without any kind of traffic, because your concentration will be heavily involved in the manoeuvre. There are two ways of doing it. Either one involves four steps, four changes of weight. Follow the diagrams carefully. In method 'A' you are facing the other way when half way through the manoeuvre. In both versions you are back where you started by the end, though on the far end of the board.

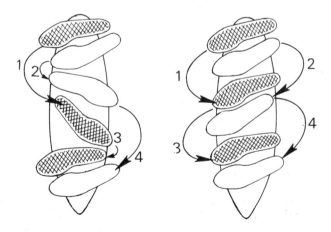

Walking the board

Pirouette Pretty, and pretty hard. You want to jump up and spin your body without disturbing the board. In fact, you hardly want to jump up at all, just around. Try 180 degrees at first, because you need to be pretty hot to make 360.

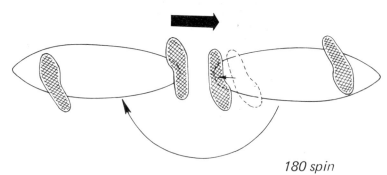

180 spin

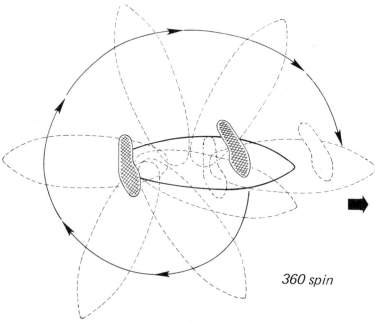

360 spin

Spins Again, aim to master a 180 degree spin before you tackle 360s, which are very impressive. This time, you take the board with you. As in a high kick turn, the rear foot moves to the tail of

Pirouette

the board, the front foot forward of the middle. Wind your upper body up by giving it a half turn in the opposite direction to that in which you are going to spin. Weight down on the tail, the nose wheels lift, you swing forcefully round, using your arms as well as your body.

Landing a nose helicopter

Half way through a 360 spin

When you think you have become about the second best skateboarder in the world, try doing the same thing from the nose of the board instead of the tail. It is about ten times as difficult, and is known as a nose helicopter.

Gorilla grip You need to be a real nut to try this, so don't. There are reckoned to be two men in the States who do it, and that is the only reason it is mentioned here. They skate barefoot, riding with their feet turned out so the toes grip the nose and the tail of the board. Then they jump, taking the board with them, and one of them can clear a dustbin on its side. They must be mad.

45

6 Heading for a fall

There is no point in pretending that, however much pleasure this sport gives you, it is not going to give you some pain as well. You will fall. You will hurt yourself. Young people can take a bruise and a graze in their stride, and you seldom see a skateboarder put off by anything as petty as that. But if the graze is too deep, and the bruise is a sprain, and at the heart of the whole thing there is a broken bone, you are going to have to lay off skateboarding for a while. As that great speed man Denis Shufeldt said, 'A feeling of freeness comes from motion sports, and this can overshadow the awareness of possible injury.'

The United States Consumer Product Safety Commission, in their 1975 survey, reported that skates, skateboards and scooters, lumped together, accounted for fewer than 3 per cent of the accidents they investigated, placing those sports twenty-fifth in the league, based on the number and the severity of the accidents. (Ten times as many were caused by bicycles, which were top of the black list, and more than twice as many would you believe, were caused by beds!) Hospitals in southern California, the home of skateboarding, said that in the summer of '75 (the first season of the new boom) there was a 100 per cent increase in their treatment of teenagers with broken limbs. High among the casualties were those suffering from what became known as 'skateboarder's elbow' — a fracture of the 'funny bone'.

Nothing more should have to be said to convince you that it makes sense to wear elbow pads — old socks held on with crepe bandages, something like that. There is so little flesh on an elbow that it is incessantly in the front line of assault, a sure target in the 'falling forward' accident that is the usual result of overbalancing. The palms of the hands are torn, the wrist bruised (or broken), the forearm grazed, the elbow cracked. Waste no time in learning how to fall so as to reduce impact injury.

You must cut down the length of time the impact position is maintained. The longer the big bone of your forearm is forced against the little bones of your wrist, the more likely something is to break. So if you do take a heavy fall by sticking your hands flat on the ground, let that be only the beginning of a fluid movement that rolls your body over in a diagonal somersault. Your head must be tucked under and to one side, and the shoulder of the other side is the pivot of a roll that passes across the length of your back and your backside. Try it out on the grass, or better still on the gym mat — it's the basis of most judo break-falls. Learn to give the fleshy parts of your body the hard treatment, and try to keep the bony ones (particularly your head) off the ground.

There are three other things you can do to reduce the likelihood, or the severity, of injury when you fall. Do you remember from an early chapter that crouching down on the board (for speeding) lowers the centre of gravity, which makes you more stable? Obviously, it also leaves you less far to fall. If you know you are going, try to get as low as possible before you actually come off, which also makes it easier for you to go into the impact-breaking roll. Next, do not stiffen against the impact. A rigid body will suffer far more than a relaxed one — that is why sleepwalkers can sometimes fall from bedroom windows without much harm. Lastly, and always, make sure you ride the board leaning slightly forward rather than backward. A back fall is much more difficult to cushion and usually leads to more severe injury.

Maybe with all your precautions, and despite your moderate speeds and sensible clothing and altogether admirable behaviour on a skateboard, you will still find yourself a minor casualty. If you do (and the odds are you will), take a little sensible advice from the British Red Cross Society.

Always clean a graze; wash out the dirt that has been forced into the skin, with some mild disinfectant if possible, under a running tap if not. Dry it, and cover the graze if it is a nasty one, otherwise the dirt will get in again and you will find yourself with a septic wound.

If you seem to have sprained a wrist or an ankle, by falling awkwardly on it, soak a handkerchief in cold water and tie it or hold it on. Get to a doctor as soon as you can, or at least go home for help. Fractures: strangely enough, you cannot always tell when you have broken a bone, specially one of the small bones of the wrist or ankle; that is why medical advice on what you think is a sprain is necessary. If you have had a bad fall, particularly one in which your arm or leg has been twisted under you on impact, and you find the limb either numb or very painful, please do not mess about trying to see if you can still ride a board. If it is a leg, stay sitting down and ask someone to go for help. If an arm and you feel well enough to walk, put it in some sort of sling and get yourself home, or to a hospital. Beware of kind people who want to shove you into a car: fractures are often greatly

aggravated by being mishandled. Finally, if you fall on your head and are left with a headache, or if the fall made you lose consciousness, stop skating. Go home. See a doctor.

If you are lucky, and if you are careful, you will get away without any of these horrors and enjoy your skateboarding so much you will teach it to your children.

Acknowledgments

This book could not have been written without the help of Olly Haycraft, of the Slick Willies Skateboard team in London, nor without the co-operation given by the publishers of *Skateboarder* magazine, of Dana Point, California.

The photographs are by Neil Libbert, Simon Tester, and Warren Bolster (courtesy of *Skateboarder* magazine). The drawings are by Elizabeth Winson and Rocky Brann. The design is by Tony Birks-Hay.